Charles Simeon on *The Excellency of the Liturgy*

Andrew Atherstone

Tutor in History and Doctrine, and Latimer research fellow,
at Wycliffe Hall, Oxford.

Contents

The cover picture is a contemporary aquatint of Charles Simeon preaching at the University Church in Cambridge in the early 1810s, published by the artist Robert Dighton (1751-1814).

First published October 2011
© Andrew Atherstone 2011

ISSN 0951-2667
ISBN 978-1-84825-138-0

1

A Form of Sound Words

In 1812, Charles Simeon, the leading evangelical clergyman in the Church of England, published a remarkable statement. Laying down the gauntlet to his critics, he declared:

> I desire every thing I ever have written, or ever shall write, to be brought to *that test*, THE LITURGY OF THE CHURCH OF ENGLAND; persuaded as I am of its perfect conformity to the Holy Scriptures.[1]

While most evangelical authors insist on being judged on the basis of the Bible alone, *sola scriptura*, Simeon was prepared for his teaching also to be measured by the doctrine of the *Book of Common Prayer*. It became, in this sense, his secondary rule of faith. With his Anglican credentials under scrutiny in the 1810s, Simeon's reply was that he and his evangelical contemporaries in the Church of England could demonstrate their heartfelt loyalty to the Liturgy of the national church. The Prayer Book was one of the keystones of Simeon's Anglican evangelical identity, influencing both his devotional discipline and his theological framework. He often conversed and preached about the Liturgy, and spent considerable effort trying to instil in his hearers a deep love for its prayers

---

1 Charles Simeon, *The Excellency of the Liturgy in Four Discourses … to which is prefixed An Answer to Dr Marsh's Inquiry* (Smith, Cambridge, 1812), p. 34.

and its principles. He considered his sermon series on *The Excellency of the Liturgy* to be amongst the most significant he ever delivered.

Simeon's impact upon the Church of England was considerable.[2] As minister of Holy Trinity, Cambridge from his ordination in 1782 until his death in 1836, he was instrumental in the rapid rise of evangelicalism to become a dominant religious force in Hanoverian and Victorian Britain. Alongside William Wilberforce and other members of the 'Clapham Sect', Simeon was the figurehead and guiding light of the Anglican evangelical movement. He mentored generations of undergraduates at Cambridge, helped to launch new evangelical organizations like the Church Missionary Society and the British and Foreign Bible Society, and consolidated evangelical parochial ministry through his Simeon Trust. He is best remembered as a preacher and his magnum opus of sermon outlines, *Horae Homileticae*, fills 21 volumes.[3] In the famous verdict of Thomas Babington Macaulay, an undergraduate at Trinity College in the early 1820s:

> As to Simeon, if you knew what his authority and influence were, and how they extended from Cambridge to the most remote corners of England, you would allow that his real sway in the Church was far greater than that of any primate.[4]

Yet despite numerous books and doctoral theses examining Simeon's life and ministry, his views on the Liturgy of the Church of England, which were a central part of his theological and ecclesiological thought, have been ignored. His sermons on *The Excellency of the Liturgy* are largely

---

2 The standard biographies are Handley C. G. Moule, *Charles Simeon* (Methuen, London, 1892) and Hugh Evan Hopkins, *Charles Simeon of Cambridge* (Hodder and Stoughton, London, 1977).

3 On Simeon as a preacher, see especially Charles Smyth, *The Art of Preaching: A Practical Survey of Preaching in the Church of England 747–1939* (SPCK, London, 1940), pp. 174–201; Hugh Evan Hopkins, *Charles Simeon: Preacher Extraordinary* (Grove Liturgical Study No.18, Grove Books, Nottingham, 1979).

4 G. O. Trevelyan, *Life and Letters of Lord Macaulay* (2 vols, Longmans, Green & Co, London, 1876), vol. 1, p. 68.

forgotten and seldom read. Apart from two brief articles by Douglas Webster and John Scrivener, Simeon's attitude to the Prayer Book has escaped scholarly assessment.[5] Therefore this Joint Liturgical Study aims to help redress the balance. It offers an extended abridgement of *The Excellency of the Liturgy*, with a brief historical commentary to set those sermons in their context.

Simeon's Prayer Book Spirituality

Simeon's engagement with the Liturgy of the Church of England was deeply interwoven with the formation of his evangelical spirituality. As a young undergraduate at King's College he experienced dramatic evangelical conversion on Easter Sunday 1779, following a crisis of conscience about receiving holy communion which was required under college statute. An immediate consequence of this changed perspective was a new love for the Prayer Book Liturgy. Simeon recalled in his autobiography that although the services at King's College Chapel were 'almost at all times … very irreverently performed', nevertheless the Liturgy now became 'marrow and fatness to me' (Psalm 63.5). He observed:

> This is proof to me, that the deadness and formality experienced in the worship of the Church, arise far more from the low state of our graces, than from any defect in our Liturgy; if only we had our hearts deeply penitent and contrite, I know from my experience at this hour, that no prayers in the world could be better suited to our wants, or more delightful to our souls.[6]

This high praise for the *Book of Common Prayer* was to become a

---

5 Douglas Webster, 'Charles Simeon and the Liturgy'. *Theology* vol. 54 (August 1951), pp. 296–301; John Scrivener, 'Charles Simeon and the Prayer Book'. *Faith and Worship* no. 57 (Michaelmas 2005), pp. 41–6.

6 Simeon's Memoir (1813), quoted in William Carus (ed.), *Memoirs of the Life of the Rev. Charles Simeon … with a Selection from his Writings and Correspondence* (Hatchard, London, 1847), p. 10.

dominant motif in Simeon's teaching. For example, Abner William Brown (undergraduate at Queens' College, Cambridge from 1827 to 1830) records in his notes from Simeon's sermon classes and 'conversation parties' several striking aphorisms said to have fallen from his mentor's lips: 'The Bible first, the Prayer Book next, and all other books and doings in subordination to both' and 'The finest sight short of heaven would be a whole congregation using the prayers of the Liturgy in the true spirit of them.'[7] Simeon claimed that no other human composition was so free from fault as the *Book of Common Prayer*,[8] and his love for it was multiplied by comparison with Presbyterian worship which he experienced during preaching tours in Scotland:

> I have on my return to the use of our Liturgy been perfectly astonished at the vast superiority of our mode of worship, and felt it an inestimable privilege that we possess a form of sound words, so adapted in every respect to the wants and desires of all who would worship God in spirit and in truth.[9]

Simeon's crucicentric spirituality was a typical evangelical emphasis,[10] and James Gordon suggests that this was due in part to his immersion in the Prayer Book, where the cross of Christ is a dominant theme:

> An Easter conversion repeatedly recalled, and annually celebrated within a Church which had produced a rich liturgy, woven around the great redemptive events of the Christian year, encouraged Simeon's spirituality to focus on Christ crucified, risen and experienced.[11]

---

7 Abner William Brown, *Recollections of the Conversations Parties of the Rev. Charles Simeon* (Hamilton, Adams & Co, London, 1863), pp. 12, 221.

8 Quoted in Moule, *Charles Simeon*, p. 85.

9 Simeon's Memoir (1813), quoted in Carus, *Memoirs*, pp. 113–14.

10 David Bebbington, *Evangelicalism in Modern Britain: A History from the 1730s to the 1980s* (Routledge, London, 1989), pp. 14–17; Ian Randall, *What a Friend We Have in Jesus: The Evangelical Tradition* (Darton, Longman and Todd, London, 2005), pp. 93–110.

11 James M. Gordon, *Evangelical Spirituality: From the Wesleys to John Stott* (SPCK, London, 1991), p. 96.

This life-long emphasis upon salvation through Christ, leading to thankful praise, comes across clearly in a private memorandum written by Simeon at the age of 60 to explain his inward experience since his undergraduate conversion:

> There are but two objects that I have ever desired for these forty years to behold; the one is, my own vileness; and the other is, the glory of God in the face of Jesus Christ: and I have always thought that they should be viewed together … This is the religion that pervades the whole Liturgy, and particularly the Communion Service; and this makes the Liturgy inexpressibly sweet to me. The repeated cries to each Person of the ever-adorable Trinity for mercy, are not at all too frequent or too fervent for me; nor is the confession in the Communion Service too strong for me; nor the 'Te Deum', nor the ascriptions of glory after the Lord's Supper, 'Glory be to God on high, &c' too exalted for me; the praise all through savours of *adoration*; and the adoration of humility. And this shews what men of God the framers of our Liturgy were, and what I pant, and long, and strive to be. This makes the Liturgy as superior to all modern compositions, as the work of a Philosopher on any deep subject is to that of a school-boy, who understands scarcely anything about it.[12]

As Gordon accurately concludes, 'Simeon preferred familiar order, well-loved prayers and the freedom of mind and heart to assimilate truth and commune with God without the intrusion of hortatory voices.'[13]

On some occasions it almost seemed as if Simeon placed the Liturgy on a par with preaching. Indeed, as Hughes Oliphant Old observes in his multi-volume history of homiletics, Simeon, like other Anglican evangelicals of his day, regarded preaching as worship. It was not primarily didactic but doxological – its aim was to exalt Christ.[14]

---

12 Simeon's Memorandum (1819), quoted in Carus, *Memoirs*, pp. 519–20.

13 Gordon, *Evangelical Spirituality*, p. 104.

14 Hughes Oliphant Old, *Reading and Preaching of the Scriptures* (7 vols, Eerdmans, Grand Rapids, 1998–2010), vol. 5, pp. 576–7.

Conversely, he also regarded public worship as a form of preaching – the prayers of the church were a proclamation of the gospel. Therefore, it was not just preaching that was a converting ordinance. In Simeon's view, the Liturgy could be too. For example, in the spring of 1807 he heard of two people who were spiritually 'awakened' by the Prayer Book, including the brother of Sir James Graham (Tory MP) who had been converted by a line from the Litany, 'From everlasting damnation, good Lord, deliver us'. Simeon noted in his diary, 'Surely the Liturgy is of more service than is generally imagined.'[15] Nevertheless, Simeon still looked to the preaching of Scripture to breathe life into the Liturgy. As he said at one of his 'conversation parties':

> It is true that the Word of God is in the Liturgy, and constantly read; and when it is properly read, it may communicate much good, even when the pulpit is poorly filled. But, in point of fact, when the pulpit is poorly filled, the reading-desk is generally so also.[16]

The happiest combination was for a parish to be served by a minister who loved both the Bible and the Prayer Book, who was energetic both in preaching and in public prayer. Simeon's sermons on *The Excellency of the Liturgy* demonstrate his desire for both these virtues. Yet he was not the only evangelical to preach on this topic. In fact, his famous exaltation of the Prayer Book was part of a long Anglican evangelical tradition.

Simeon's Predecessors and Contemporaries on the Prayer Book

Ever since the *Book of Common Prayer* first came into existence, there had been a constant stream of treatises and sermons expounding its significance and extolling its virtues. One of the most enduring was William Beveridge's *Sermon Concerning the Excellency and Usefulness of the Common-Prayer*, preached at the re-opening of St Peter's, Cornhill, in

---

15 Simeon's Diary, 2 April 1807, quoted in Carus, *Memoirs*, p. 223.
16 Brown, *Recollections*, p. 220.

1681. It quickly became a religious classic and was widely read throughout the eighteenth century and into the early nineteenth century – often republished by the SPCK, it reached a thirty-sixth edition in 1773 and a forty-fourth edition in 1824. Other standard authorities from the late Stuart period, which were still in circulation a century later, included Thomas Comber's *A Companion to the Temple; or, A Help to Devotion in the Use of the Common Prayer* (1676); Thomas Bennet's *Paraphrase with Annotations upon the Book of Common Prayer* (1708); William Nicholls' *Comment on the Book of Common-Prayer* (1710); Matthew Hole's *Practical Discourses on All the Parts and Offices of the Liturgy of the Church of England* (1714–19) and Charles Wheatly's *The Church of England Man's Companion; or A Rational Illustration of the Harmony, Excellency, and Usefulness of the Book of Common Prayer* (1710). Wheatly's work was so popular that it remained in print up until the 1860s.

However, Charles Simeon could reasonably claim at the start of the nineteenth century that it was the evangelical clergy, more than anyone else, who had the habit of writing and preaching expositions on the Church of England's Liturgy. As an early example, he pointed back to Samuel Walker (1714–61), minister of Truro in Cornwall from 1746 until his death.[17] Simeon considered Walker's sermons to be 'the best in the English language'.[18] When Walker drew up orders of service for the evangelical societies he established in his parish (the eighteenth-century equivalent of the Bible Study or discipleship group), it was to the Prayer Book he went for his material, which set them apart as distinct from similar Methodist gatherings.[19] Other early evangelicals such as William Grimshaw, John Berridge, William Romaine, Thomas Scott, John Newton and Henry Venn were likewise wedded to the Church of England's Liturgy. Sometimes it could be put to controversial as well as devotional use. Augustus Toplady (1740–78), for example, turned to the *Book of Common Prayer* in his combat against Arminianism in order to

---

17 Simeon, *The Excellency of the Liturgy*, pp. 36–7.

18 Brown, *Recollections*, p. 320.

19 G. C. B. Davies, *The Early Cornish Evangelicals, 1735–60: A Study of Walker of Truro and Others* (SPCK, London, 1951), pp. 68–9.

justify the Calvinist position, in his posthumously published *The Liturgy of the Church of England Explained and Vindicated* (1800).[20]

The second generation of Anglican evangelicals were equally enthusiastic in their admiration for the Prayer Book, perhaps even more so. Amongst Simeon's own contemporaries, the outstanding expositor of the Liturgy was Thomas Biddulph (1763–1838), the leading evangelical clergyman in Bristol.[21] During 1798, he delivered a series of 12 evening lectures at St Werburgh's, Bristol, in which he examined Morning Prayer and Evening Prayer in detail, from the introductory sentences to the general thanksgiving. They were soon published as *Essays on Some Select Parts of the Liturgy of the Church of England*, lauding the 'multifarious excellency of our church-liturgy'.[22] Biddulph told his congregation that he had chosen to preach on this theme out of nothing less than 'a desire to promote your everlasting salvation'.[23] He believed that the truths exhibited in the *Book of Common Prayer* were 'of unspeakable importance to all persons in every age' and hoped that his hearers would every day 'be animated more and more by that spirit of vital Godliness, which our liturgy breathes through all her varied forms of devotion.'[24]

Simeon's exalted views of the Liturgy were in part derived from Biddulph, and the parallels between some of their expressions are striking. Biddulph identified three particular 'excellencies' of the Liturgy, the first and most important of which was its orthodoxy and its wholehearted agreement 'with the one unerring standard of all Divine truth'. With the eighteenth-century Deists firmly in view, he proclaimed: 'Our liturgy is not like a nose of wax, that may be adapted to every face

---

20 Augustus Toplady, *The Liturgy of the Church of England Explained and Vindicated, so as to Appear in Perfect Harmony with the Scriptures, and Very Far Distant from the Arminian System* (Barker, London, 1800).

21 On Biddulph, see L. P. Fox, *The Work of the Reverend Thomas Tregenna Biddulph* (unpublished PhD thesis, Cambridge University, 1953).

22 Thomas T. Biddulph, *Essays on Some Select Parts of the Liturgy of the Church of England* (Pine, Bristol, 1798), p. 338.

23 *Ibid.*, p. iii.

24 *Ibid.*, pp. ix, xi.

... its language on all the fundamental doctrines of Christianity is clear and decisive.' Any Socinian or Pelagian clergyman was 'condemned out of his own mouth' when using the Prayer Book and Biddulph rejoiced in this liturgical bulwark against the intrusion of doctrinal error into the Church of England.[25] The second 'excellency' he identified was the Liturgy's variety, suitable for every worshipper whatever their personal circumstances, whether guilt-ridden or praise-filled. The third 'excellency' was the Prayer Book's deep spirituality:

> Nothing is to be found therein to satisfy the conscience of the formalist and Pharisee; but, on the contrary, every thing that is calculated to awaken attention to the necessity of the worship of the heart, communion with God, and real delight in His service. ... the worship of our church is adapted exclusively to the use of those, who desire and expect to enjoy on earth, in the courts of the Lord's house, that which may afford them a foretaste of, and fit them for more refined and exalted pleasures at God's right-hand for evermore.[26]

In 1803, the newly founded *Christian Observer* (mouthpiece of the Clapham Sect) urged other evangelical clergymen to follow Biddulph's example with sets of practical sermons expounding the 'unrivalled merits' of the Prayer Book:

> He ... who labours to enable the ignorant to comprehend the Liturgy, to persuade the careless to examine it, and to awaken and stimulate the formalist to feel it, certainly undertakes a very necessary work, and deserves great commendation. He does honour to the Church, by exemplifying one of its greatest excellencies; and confers an important benefit upon its members, by furnishing them with the means of increasing both the rationality and spirituality of their devotions ...[27]

---

25 *Ibid.*, pp. 22–3.
26 *Ibid.*, p. 25.
27 *Christian Observer* vol. 2 (September 1803), p. 548.

The journal insisted that such a sermon series would 'afford an opportunity of saying almost every thing which a minister of the Gospel ought to teach, and which a hearer of the Gospel ought to learn'.[28] Over the next few years, several evangelical ministers responded to the challenge. One of them was Thomas Rogers (1760–1832), headmaster of Wakefield Grammar School, for whom a Sunday evening lectureship had been established in 1801 at Wakefield parish church. He delivered 31 lectures expounding Morning Prayer, aiming to give his congregation 'a more intimate and spiritual acquaintance' with the Liturgy, its 'excellency and utility', and to demonstrate that it had 'no other foundation than the doctrines and practice of the Apostles and Prophets, Jesus Christ himself being the chief corner stone'.[29] Rogers declared:

> These excellent compositions of the Common Prayer, have a strong claim to your serious attention, not only for the plainness and simplicity of their style, and the admirable order in which they are arranged; but for their direct tendency to produce and establish in you that humility and spirituality of mind which every real Christian would wish to possess, when approaching the throne of Grace. If you are earnestly studying to enter into the real spirit of them, you will find them more suitable for expressing your sentiments of religious obligation and dependence, in the Divine presence, than any human composition that has yet been attempted.[30]

He hoped his lectures would give his congregation 'enlarged views of the true excellence, and real worth' of the Church of England's Liturgy, 'which has been blessed to the edification, comfort, and salvation of multitudes'.[31] Rogers followed his series on Morning Prayer with another 37 lectures through 1804 and 1805 expounding the Litany, 'that truly

---

28 *Ibid.*, p. 550.
29 Thomas Rogers, *Lectures Delivered in the Parish Church of Wakefield* (3rd edition, Longman, London, 1816), part 1, pp. iv, xi.
30 *Ibid.*, part 1, pp. iv–v.
31 *Ibid.*, part 1, pp. 2–3.

excellent and affecting part of our Church-service'.[32] Meanwhile Biddulph continued with his liturgical sermons in Bristol. Over a period of a year, he preached 83 sermons expounding each of the Prayer Book collects for Sundays and holy days, published in three volumes. He particularly delighted in this theme, because whereas other ministers were now preaching about Morning and Evening Prayer, the collects remained 'untrodden ground'.[33]

Sermons on the *Book of Common Prayer* were also a popular topic at archidiaconal visitations. For example, Basil Woodd (1760–1831), the evangelical rector of Drayton Beauchamp in Buckinghamshire, expounded the services of Morning and Evening Prayer before his fellow clergymen at a local visitation in 1810. The sermon was published as *The Excellence of the Liturgy*, and Simeon believed it should be bound up with Beveridge's classic on *The Excellency and Usefulness of the Common-Prayer*, and placed 'in the hands of every Clergyman in the kingdom'.[34] Woodd spoke of the Church of England's great privilege 'to possess an established form of worship, strictly corresponding with the doctrines of the Holy Scriptures, glowing with the devotional spirit, which they breath[e], and enforcing the practical purity, which they enjoin'.[35] He encouraged his hearers to view the Prayer Book

> as an epitome of the Christian Religion, and as a standard of pastoral instruction. ... The Liturgy not only is presented to us as a form of prayer, but it is at the same time a standing Christian sermon, delivered every returning sabbath, in upwards of ten thousand Churches; diffusing an atmosphere of religious knowledge throughout the kingdom; establishing a pure and unsophisticated standard of evangelical truth; so combined, that no man can duly attend to the

---

32 *Ibid.*, part 2, p. 2.

33 Thomas T. Biddulph, *Practical Essays on the Collects in the Liturgy of the Church of England for Sundays and Other Holidays*, attached to *Practical Essays on the Morning and Evening Services of the Church of England* (2nd edition, Longman, London, 1810), vol. 1, p. 264.

34 Simeon, *The Excellency of the Liturgy*, p. 38.

35 Basil Woodd, *The Excellence of the Liturgy* (Bridgewater, London, 1810), pp. 4–5.

service, and remain ignorant of the nature of the Gospel. Let us, my reverend brethren, who are ministers of our venerable establishment, be ourselves stedfast in our attachment to its constitution, doctrine, and discipline. Let our discourses from the pulpit breathe the same spirit, exhibit the same distinguishing truths, and recommend the same purity of practice.[36]

One of the favourite Bible texts chosen by preachers when extolling the Liturgy was 2 Timothy 1.13: 'Hold fast the form of sound words'. Beveridge, for example, had proclaimed: 'if ever there was *A Form of sound Words*, composed by Men since the Apostles Times, our *Common-Prayer* may justly deserve that Title'.[37] This Bible verse was adopted by Biddulph as the slogan for his *Essays*, and by Woodd as the motto for his visitation sermon. It was also adopted by George Gaskin for his sermon at St Mary's, Islington, on *The English Liturgy: A 'Form of Sound Words'* (1806), and by Charles Musgrave (vicar of Whitkirk in Yorkshire) for his visitation sermon *On the Excellence of the Liturgy* (1824).

When it came to family devotions, there was a raft of manuals which looked to the *Book of Common Prayer* for prayers and collects which could be used in the home with children and servants. Amongst the most enduring eighteenth-century works, often republished, were Edmund Gibson's *Family-Devotion: or, A Plain Exhortation to Morning and Evening Prayer in Families* (1705), William Mason's *The Christian's Companion for the Sabbath; Suited for the Family or Closet* (1771) and James Bean's *Family Worship: A Course of Morning and Evening Prayers* (1796). In this area too, evangelicals played a prominent part. For example, Samuel Knight (1759–1827), the evangelical vicar of Halifax, published *Forms of Prayer, For the Use of Christian Families* (1791), which went through 16 editions in his lifetime and was in its thirtieth edition by 1844. Likewise the posthumously published *Family Prayers* by Henry

---

36 *Ibid.*, pp. 23–4.
37 William Beveridge, *A Sermon Concerning the Excellency and Usefulness of the Common-Prayer* (36th edition, Beecroft, London, 1773), p. 20.

Thornton (1760–1815), evangelical philanthropist and leading light of the Clapham Sect, was an immediate best-seller and ran through 30 editions in two years.[38] Simeon himself was also keen to promote aids to family devotion, particularly those which were in accordance with the doctrine and spirit of the Prayer Book, and he issued a new edition of Benjamin Jenks' classic, *Prayers, and Offices of Devotion; for Families, and for Particular Persons, Upon Most Occasions* (1697), which gave the manual a fresh lease of life.

---

38 Henry Thornton, *Family Prayers* (Hatchard, London, 1834).

2

The Excellency of the Liturgy

Alongside his regular ministry at Holy Trinity Church, Charles Simeon was occasionally called upon to preach before the University of Cambridge at Great St Mary's. Six times between 1805 and 1831 he served as a 'select preacher' and also delivered sermons on significant local occasions like the Commemoration of Benefactors and the Cambridge Assizes. Amongst his best-known University addresses are classics such as *Evangelical and Pharisaic Righteousness Compared* (1809); *Christ Crucified, or Evangelical Religion Described* (1811); and the series entitled *Appeal to Men of Wisdom and Candour* (1815).[39] It was by his University sermons that Simeon most wanted to be judged, and in his *Horae Homileticae* he drew particular attention to his addresses on the Liturgy as demonstrating the agreement between his own views and those of the Church of England.[40]

One of Simeon's earliest University sermons, six years before his famous series on *The Excellency of the Liturgy*, also focussed upon the Prayer Book. In 1805 Herbert Marsh, the Lady Margaret Professor of Divinity, launched a fierce attack upon the 'Calvinistic' doctrines of the

---

39 Simeon's other University sermons include *On the Gospel Message* (1796), *The Fountain of Living Waters* (1809), *The True Test of Religion in the Soul* (1817); and series entitled, *The Nature and Office of the Gospel* (1824), *The Uses of the Law* (1828), *The Offices of the Holy Spirit* (1831).

40 Charles Simeon, *Horae Homileticae: or Discourses (Principally in the Form of Skeletons) Now First Digested into One Continued Series, and Forming a Commentary Upon Every Book of the Old and New Testament* (21 vols, Holdsworth and Ball, London, 1832–3), vol. 1, p. xxvii.

evangelical movement.[41] Simeon replied with a sermon entitled *The Churchman's Confession, or an Appeal to the Liturgy*. In a passionate defence against Marsh's 'false accusations', he argued that both the Bible and the Prayer Book supported evangelical doctrine. Simeon explained:

> It is true, we are not to put any human compositions on a level with the inspired volume: the Scriptures alone are the proper standard of truth; but the Articles, Homilies, and Liturgy of the Church of England are an authorized exposition of the sense in which all her members profess to understand the Scriptures. To these therefore we appeal as well as to the sacred records.[42]

Simeon focussed upon the General Confession from Morning and Evening Prayer, showing how it taught three vital but disputed truths: 'our lost estate' (the prevalence and seriousness of sin), 'the means of our recovery' (repentance and faith alone in Jesus Christ) and 'the path of duty' (the need for radical holiness). He commended the General Confession, 'that truly scriptural prayer', as a test by which to judge both public preaching and personal experience. Simeon insisted: 'As members of the Church of England we have a right to expect that the discourses of ministers shall correspond with the Liturgy of our Church.'[43]

Few could mistake the tone of aggressive defiance of this University sermon, an outspoken riposte to Professor Marsh and other anti-evangelical critics. Simeon reported to his friend John Venn (vicar of Clapham) that it 'seems to have made more stir and impression than any of my Sermons (some have said, more than all together) … O

---

41 On Marsh, see R. K. Braine, *The Life and Writings of Herbert Marsh (1757–1839)* (unpublished PhD thesis, Cambridge University, 1989); David Thompson, *Cambridge Theology in the Nineteenth Century: Enquiry, Controversy and Truth* (Ashgate, Aldershot, 2008), pp. 31–47. On Marsh's anti-Calvinism, see Arthur Pollard, 'Trap to Catch Calvinists, or Bishop Marsh's Eighty-Seven Questions', *Church Quarterly Review* vol. 162 (1961), pp. 447–54.

42 Charles Simeon, *The Churchman's Confession, or an Appeal to the Liturgy* (1805), republished in Simeon, *Horae Homileticae*, vol. 16, p. 407.

43 *Ibid.*, p. 418.

that God may be pleased to bless it to the conviction and conversion of many!'[44] The *Eclectic Review* portrayed the address in a generous light:

> The arguments are plain and incontrovertible; the spirit of meekness and calm firmness is strongly evidenced; no violence, no railing, no rant, no enthusiasm offends us here; but the cause of truth is maintained with decency and success. No man really entertaining such sentiments, can be considered in any other light than that of a true christian [*sic*], a sincere protestant, and a strict churchman.[45]

Yet by the *Orthodox Churchman's Magazine* it was slated as 'another attempt to prove the Calvinism of the Church of England ... one of the weakest we remember to have seen ... *radically* objectionable'.[46] Edward Pearson (Master of Sidney Sussex College from 1808), a regular antagonist of evangelicals in the Church of England, agreed that Simeon's sermon was an erroneous and misleading contortion of the Anglican liturgy. He complained that it had been preached

> ...with the evident design of supporting the unfounded notions, entertained by *evangelical* or *Calvinistic* divines, of the *total corruption* of human nature, and of justification and salvation by *faith only* as opposed to *obedience*, with which notions the *confession* has just as much to do as it has with the doctrine of *transubstantiation*, or *purgatory*, or any other creature of the human fancy ...[47]

In November 1811 Simeon returned to the Prayer Book liturgy as the grand theme for a new set of University sermons, preached on four successive Sundays. At first sight, their tone is more irenic than that of

---

44 Charles Simeon to John Venn, 12 December 1805, in Carus, *Memoirs*, p. 209.
45 *Eclectic Review* vol. 2, part 1 (March 1806), p. 237.
46 *Orthodox Churchman's Magazine*, vol. 10 (May 1806), pp. 386, 390.
47 *Orthodox Churchman's* Magazine, vol. 10 (June 1806), p. 415.

The Churchman's Confession. His primary purpose was no longer to defend evangelicalism against attacks by critics within the Cambridge Establishment, but to defend the Prayer Book against attacks by Dissenters and some evangelicals within the Church of England. It was also an exercise in self-defence, since in 1811 a fresh crisis was brewing in Simeon's own parish where he was accused of false teaching and irregular practices, which led to clashes with the Bishop of Ely and the University authorities.[48] Therefore *The Excellency of the Liturgy* was particularly significant as a demonstration of his Anglican credentials, and at one stage he planned to publish the sermons at the head of his *Horae Homileticae.*[49] Crowds turned out to listen, as Simeon reported to a friend: 'the audiences were very large, numbers of Masters of Arts being forced to go up into the galleries; and though the Sermons were an hour long, there was not the smallest symptom of weariness to be seen'.[50]

Although published five times between 1812 and 1832, and once widely read, Simeon's sermons on *The Excellency of the Liturgy* have fallen into obscurity. In 1959, the Inter-Varsity Fellowship published a selection of his University addresses, edited by Arthur Pollard, and these included *The Churchman's Confession* but ignored these other, more important, sermons on the Liturgy.[51] More recently, in 2003, Regent College, Van-couver, produced an anthology of Simeon's sermons introduced by John Stott and edited by James Houston, and these included *The Excellency of the Scriptures* but again ignored his sermons on *The Excellency of the Liturgy.*[52] The bulk of this chapter therefore offers a detailed summary and abridgement of their content. Sermon II is given at greater length and Sermon III almost in full, allowing Simeon to speak for himself.

---

48 On Simeon's attitude to canonical irregularities, see further, Andrew Atherstone, *Evangelical Mission and Anglican Church Order: Charles Simeon Reconsidered* (Latimer Trust, London, 2009).

49 Simeon, *The Excellency of the Liturgy*, pp. 33–4.

50 Simeon to Thomas Thomason, 3 January 1812, in Carus, *Memoirs*, p. 318.

51 Arthur Pollard (ed.), *Let Wisdom Judge: University Addresses and Sermon Outlines by Charles Simeon* (Inter-Varsity Press, London, 1959).

52 James M. Houston (ed.), *Evangelical Preaching: An Anthology of Sermons by Charles Simeon* (Regent College, Vancouver, British Columbia, 2003; first published by Multnomah Press in 1986).

Sermon I

Simeon's four sermons were all based around a short Bible passage from Deuteronomy 5.28–9: 'They have well said all that they have spoken: O that there were such an heart in them!' This text, of course, had nothing to do with the Liturgy of the Church of England. In its proper historical context, it concerned the giving of the Ten Commandments to Moses on Mount Sinai, when the Lord spoke to the assembled Israelites from 'out of the midst of the fire, of the cloud, and of the thick darkness, with a great voice'. After this terrifying theophany, the elders went to Moses and pleaded that, in future, he listen to the Lord on their behalf. The Lord responded: 'I have heard the voice of the words of this people, which they have spoken unto thee: they have well said all that they have spoken. O that there were such an heart in them …' Although Simeon was keen to talk about the Liturgy, he felt honour-bound to use his first sermon for a proper explanation of his Bible text. He proclaimed that these Old Testament events 'shadow forth the whole mystery of redemption', pointing towards the work of Jesus Christ.[53] From these verses in Deuteronomy, he argued that God wishes to find in his people a reverential fear of the Lord, a deep love of Jesus as their Mediator, and a genuine delight in his commands. Having thus expounded his text 'in its true and proper sense', he now felt at liberty in his next three sermons to expound it 'in an improper and accommodated sense'.[54]

Sermon II

Simeon opened his second sermon before the University by justifying his plan to use a verse from Deuteronomy to speak about the Liturgy of the Church of England:

The further use which we propose to make of this passage, is only in a way of accommodation; which however is abundantly sanctioned

---

53 Simeon, *The Excellency of the Liturgy*, p. 2.
54 *Ibid.*, p. 3.

by the example of the Apostles; who not unfrequently adopt the language of the Old Testament to convey their own ideas, even when it has no necessary connexion with their subject. Of course, the Liturgy of our Church was never in the contemplation of the Sacred Historian: yet, as in that we constantly address ourselves to God, and as it is a composition of unrivalled excellence, and needs only the exercise of our devout affections to render it a most acceptable service before God, we may well apply to it the commendation in our text; 'They have well said all that they have spoken: O that there were such an heart in them!'[55]

Simeon began on the defensive. Before he could extol the excellencies of the Liturgy in Sermon III, he first felt it necessary in Sermon II to vindicate its use, lamenting: 'Perhaps there never was any human composition more cavilled at, or less deserving such treatment, than our Liturgy. Nothing has been deemed too harsh to say of it.'[56] His vindication fell into three parts, that use of the Liturgy is *lawful* (that is, allowed by Scripture), *expedient*, and *acceptable to God*.

With Dissenters clearly in his sights, Simeon argued at length 'that forms of devotion are not evil in themselves.'[57] As evidence he pointed to set prayers and psalms used by the Israelites, to the Lord's Prayer, and to the ancient Christian liturgies ascribed to Saint Peter, Saint Mark and Saint James. For Dissenters to sing hymns and yet oppose liturgy was simply inconsistent:

it is worthy of observation, that those who most loudly decry the use of forms, do themselves use forms, whenever they unite in public worship. What are hymns, but forms of prayer and praise? and if it be lawful to worship God in forms of verse, is it not equally so in forms of prose?[58]

55 *Ibid.*, p. 28.
56 *Ibid.*, p. 29.
57 *Ibid.*, p. 31.
58 *Ibid.*, p. 34.

Some may play off spirit against form, but Simeon insisted that Spirit-led prayer was possible 'as much in the use of a pre-composed form, as in any extemporaneous effusions of our own'.[59] Next, he argued that the use of the Church of England's Liturgy was *expedient*:

> Here let it not be supposed that I am about to condemn those who differ from us in judgment or in practice. The Legislature has liberally conceded to all the subjects of the realm a right of choice; and God forbid that any one should wish to abridge them of it, in a matter of such high concern as the worship of Almighty God. If any think themselves more edified by extempore prayer, we rejoice that their souls are benefited, though it be not precisely in our way: but still we cannot be insensible to the advantages which we enjoy; and much less can we concede to any that the use of a prescribed form of prayer is the smallest disadvantage.
>
> We say then, that the Liturgy was of great use *at the time it was made*. At the commencement of the Reformation the most lamentable ignorance prevailed throughout the land: and even those who from their office ought to have been well instructed in the Holy Scriptures, themselves needed to be taught what were the first principles of the oracles of God. If then the pious and venerable Reformers of our Church had not provided a suitable form of prayer, the people would still in many thousands of parishes have remained in utter darkness; but by the diffusion of this sacred light throughout the land, every part of the kingdom became in a good measure irradiated with scriptural knowledge, and with saving truth. The few who were enlightened, might indeed have scattered some partial rays around them; but their light would have been only as a meteor, that passes away and leaves no permanent effect. Moreover, if their zeal and knowledge and piety had been suffered to die with them, we should have in vain sought for compositions of equal excellence from any set of governors from that day to the present hour: but by conveying to

---

59 *Ibid.*, p. 35.

posterity the impress of their own piety in stated forms of prayer, they have in them transmitted a measure of their own spirit, which, like Elijah's mantle, has descended on multitudes who have succeeded them in their high office. It is not possible to form a correct estimate of the benefit which we at this day derive from having such a standard of piety in our hands: but we do not speak too strongly if we say, that the most enlightened amongst us, of whatever denomination they may be, owe much to the existence of our Liturgy; which has been, as it were, the pillar and ground of the truth of this kingdom, and has served as fuel to perpetuate the flame, which the Lord himself, at the time of the Reformation, kindled upon our altars.

But we must go further, and say, that the use of the Liturgy is *equally expedient still*. Of course, we must not be understood as speaking of private prayer in the closet; where, though a young and inexperienced person may get help from written forms, it is desirable that every one should learn to express his own wants in his own language; because no written prayer can enter so minutely into his wants and feelings as he himself may do: but, in public, we maintain, that the use of such a form as ours is still as expedient as ever. To lead the devotions of a congregation in extempore prayer is a work for which but few are qualified.[60] An extensive knowledge of the Scriptures must be combined with fervent piety, in order to fit a person for such an undertaking: and I greatly mistake, if there be found a humble person in the world, who,

---

60 Elsewhere Simeon declared, 'If *all* men could pray at *all* times, as *some* men can *sometimes*, then indeed we might prefer extempore to pre-composed prayers' (Carus, *Memoirs*, p. 114). And: 'That there are persons capable of conducting public worship in a truly edifying manner without a form, is readily acknowledged. But the great mass of those who lead the devotions of the people (I mean not to offend any, but only to "speak the truth in love"), are far from equal to the task: and even those whose *gifts* are sufficient, find themselves too often destitute of the *grace* of prayer. They can utter words, perhaps, with fluency: but their words betray the absence of the heart: and the barrenness felt by those who speak, is diffused over all who hear. I grant that there may also be a hardness and barrenness in one who uses a pre-conceived form: but still, if that form express all that a devout spirit could wish, the persons who join in it may themselves, through the influence of the Holy Spirit, supply the unction, which the minister has failed to manifest.' ('Forms of Prayer, Good', in Simeon, *Horae Homileticae*, vol. 12, p. 435).

after engaging often in that arduous work, does not wish at times[61] that he had a suitable form prepared for him. That the constant repetition of the same form does not forcibly arrest the attention as new sentiments and expressions would do, must be confessed: but, on the other hand, the use of a well-composed form secures us against the dry, dull, tedious repetitions which are but too frequently the fruits of extemporaneous devotions. Only let any person be in a devout frame, and he will be far more likely to have his soul elevated to heaven by the Liturgy of the Established Church, than he will by the generality of prayers which he would hear in other places of worship: and, if any one complain that he cannot enter into the spirit of them, let him only examine his frame of mind when engaged in extemporaneous prayers, whether in public, or in his own family; and he will find, that his formality is not confined to the service of the Church, but is the sad fruit and consequence of his own weakness and corruption.

Here it may not be amiss to rectify the notions which are frequently entertained of spiritual edification. Many, if their imaginations are pleased, and their spirits elevated, are ready to think, that they have been greatly edified: and this error is at the root of that preference which they give to extempore prayer, and the indifference which they manifest towards the prayers of the Established Church. But real edification consists in humility of mind, and in being led to a more holy and consistent walk with God: and one atom of such a spirit is more valuable than all the animal fervour that ever was excited. It is with *solid truths*, and not with *fluent words*, that we are to be impressed: and if we can desire from our hearts the things which we pray for in our public forms, we need never regret, that our fancy was not gratified, or our animal spirits raised, by the delusive charms of novelty.[62]

Continuing this theme, Simeon argued, thirdly, that the use of the Liturgy was *acceptable to God*:

---

61 The third edition of 1816 has 'at all times'; Charles Simeon, *The Excellency of the Liturgy* (3rd edition, Cadell and Davies, London, 1816), p. 30.

62 Simeon, *The Excellency of the Liturgy* (1812), pp. 36–40.

The words of our texts are sufficient to shew us, that God does not look at fine words and fluent expressions, but at the heart. The Israelites had 'well said all that they had spoken': but whilst God acknowledged that, he added, 'O that there were such *an heart* in them!' If there be humility and contrition in our supplications, it will make no difference with God, whether they be extemporaneous or pre-composed. Can any doubt whether, if we were to address our heavenly Father in the words which Christ himself has taught us, we should be accepted of him, provided we uttered the different petitions from our hearts? As little doubt then is there that in the use of the Liturgy also we shall be accepted, if only we draw nigh to God with our hearts as well as with our lips. The prayer of faith, whether with or without a form, shall never go forth in vain. And there are thousands at this day who can attest from their own experience, that they have often found God as present with them in the use of the public services of our Church, as ever they did in their secret chambers.[63]

Having thus vindicated the use of the Church of England's Liturgy in general terms, Simeon proceeded to defend it against particular objections which troubled the consciences of some Anglican ministers and ordinands. He began:

To notice all the expressions which captious men have cavilled at, would be a waste of time. But there are one or two which with tender minds have considerable weight, and have not only prevented many worthy men from entering into the Church, but do at this hour press upon the consciences of many, who in all other things approve and admire the public formularies of the Church. A great portion of this present assembly are educating with a view to the ministry in the Establishment; and, if I may be able in any little measure to satisfy their minds, or to remove a stumbling-block out of their way, I shall think that I have made a good use of the opportunity which is thus

---

63 *Ibid.*, p. 41.

afforded to me. A more essential service I can scarcely render unto any of my younger brethren, or indeed to the Establishment itself, than by meeting fairly the difficulties which occur to their minds, and which are too often successfully urged by the enemies of our Church, to the embarrassing of conscientious minds, and to the drawing away of many, who might have laboured comfortably and successfully in this part of our Lord's vineyard.[64]

The two popular objections which Simeon dealt with in detail, were the Burial Service's confidence in 'sure and certain hope of the resurrection to eternal life', pronounced even over some who may have died in their sins; and the Baptism Service's declaration that baptized infants are 'regenerate'. Timothy Stunt and Grayson Carter have shown that objections to these parts of the *Book of Common Prayer* were a contributory factor in the flurry of evangelical secessions from the Church of England in the early nineteenth century, both in the mid-1810s in the south-west of England (the so-called 'Western Schism') and again at Oxford in the early 1830s.[65] For example, Charles Brenton (curate of Stadhampton near Oxford) refused in 1831 to read the Burial Service over a notorious drunkard who had been the parish-clerk for 40 years. He preached a fiery sermon defending his actions, proclaiming that it was absurd, impious, wicked, blasphemous and hypocritical to use the Prayer Book funeral liturgy for 'baptized infidels', and announced to the congregation his intention to resign his ministry and leave the Church.[66] Yet in *The Excellency of the Liturgy*, Simeon argued that these troublesome Prayer Book expressions were no stronger than some used

---

64 *Ibid.*, pp. 42–3.

65 Timothy Stunt, *From Awakening to Secession: Radical Evangelicals in Switzerland and Britain 1815–35* (T & T Clark, Edinburgh, 2000), chs 10–11; Grayson Carter, *Anglican Evangelicals: Protestant Secessions from the* Via Media, *c.1800–1850* (Oxford University Press, Oxford, 2001), chs 4, 7.

66 Charles Brenton, *A Sermon on Revelation XIV.13 Tending to Shew the Absurdity and Impiety of the Promiscuous Use of the Church Burial Service* (Baxter, Oxford, 1831). See further, Andrew Atherstone, *Oxford's Protestant Spy: The Controversial Career of Charles Golightly* (Paternoster, Milton Keynes, 2007), pp. 16–21.

by the apostles in the New Testament, and that those who had scruples over the Church of England's Liturgy must feel even more uncomfortable when reading the epistles of Saint Paul or Saint Peter – such as the apostolic statements that 'as many of you as have been baptized into Christ have put on Christ' (Galatians 3.27) or 'baptism doth also now save us' (1 Peter 3.21). In particular, he appealed against an overly-systematized approach to theological language:

There is one circumstance in the formation of our Liturgy which is not sufficiently adverted to. The persons who composed it were men of a truly Apostolic spirit: unfettered by party prejudices, they endeavoured to speak in all things precisely as the Scriptures speak: they did not indulge in speculations and metaphysical reasonings; nor did they presume to be wise above what is written: they laboured to speak the truth, the whole truth, in love: and they cultivated in the highest degree that candour, that simplicity, and that charity, which so eminently characterize all the Apostolic writings. ...

Let me then speak the truth before God: Though I am no Arminian, I do think that the refinements of Calvin have done great harm in the Church: they have driven multitudes from the plain, and popular way of speaking used by the inspired Writers, and have made them unreasonably and unscripturally squeamish in their modes of expression; and I conceive that, the less addicted any person is to systematic accuracy, the more he will accord with the inspired Writers, and the more he will approve of the views of our Reformers. I do not mean however to say, that a slight alteration in two or three instances would not be an improvement; since it would take off a burthen from many minds, and supersede the necessity of laboured explanations: but I do mean to say, that there is no such objection to these expressions as to deter any conscientious person from giving his unfeigned assent and consent to the Liturgy altogether,[67] or from using

---

67 The 1662 Act of Uniformity, still in force in 1811, required every Church of England clergyman to declare his 'unfeigned assent and consent to all and everything contained and prescribed in and by' the *Book of Common Prayer*.

the particular expressions which we have been endeavouring to explain.[68]

Simeon gave similar reassurances to the undergraduates at his 'conversation parties', as recorded by Abner William Brown. Simeon argued that the Prayer Book authors adopted New Testament terminology, not some partisan theological system: 'God has not revealed His truth in a system; the Bible has no system as such. Lay aside system and fly to the Bible; receive its words with simple submission, and without an eye to any system. Be Bible Christians, and not system Christians.'[69] Concerning the Prayer Book statements on baptismal regeneration, he asked: 'Why would you interpret the words of uninspired writers more strictly than those of Scripture? ... Why quarrel with it, therefore, for being too closely like the Scripture phraseology?'[70] Concerning the controversial words 'I absolve you' in the Prayer Book liturgy for the Visitation of the Sick, Simeon appealed for a similar breadth of interpretation:

We allow a certain latitude in interpreting even the words of inspired writers, and do not interpret their words literally (as in the sacrament, – 'This is my body'). Why deny a like latitude to fallible man, whose aim in framing our services has been to keep as close as possible to Scripture, and to that alone?[71]

Likewise in the preface to his *Horae Homileticae*, the preacher declared:

Where the Inspired Writers speak in unqualified terms, he thinks himself at liberty to do the same; judging, that they need no instruction from *him* how to propagate the truth. He is content to sit

---

68 Simeon, *The Excellency of the Liturgy* (1812), pp. 43, 51–2.
69 Brown, *Recollections*, p. 269.
70 *Ibid.*, p. 233.
71 *Ibid.*, p. 210.

as a *learner* at the feet of the holy Apostles, and has no ambition to teach them how they ought to have spoken.[72]

In his second sermon on *The Excellency of the Liturgy*, Simeon concluded by replying to the popular objection that the Liturgy necessarily breeds formality. This was a particular difficulty in Cambridge, where undergraduates were obliged to attend chapel twice daily, but were notorious for their disruptive behaviour and inattention. V. H. H. Green comments on Cambridge at this period that 'In general the religious life of the University was somewhat Laodicean. ... Nor is there any evidence that the religious character of the University in any marked fashion affected the morals or manners of its members.'[73] In a debate in the House of Commons in 1834, Viscount Palmerston (who had been an undergraduate at St John's College, Cambridge 1803–6, and served as MP for Cambridge University 1811–31) lent his support to calls for a relaxation of the rules governing compulsory attendance at Anglican worship. He asked:

> Was it either essential or expedient, that young men should be compelled to rush from their beds every morning to prayers, unwashed, unshaved, and half dressed; or, in the evening, from their wine to chapel, and from chapel back again to their wine? By such a course, the interests of the Church and true religious feeling could not be really served or advanced.[74]

Into that context of formal University religion, Simeon proclaimed in *The Excellency of the Liturgy*:

> We have before acknowledged that the repetition of a form is less likely to arrest the attention than that which is novel: but we by no means concede that it necessarily generates formality: on the

---

72 Simeon, *Horae Homileticae*, p. xxiv.
73 V. H. H. Green, *Religion at Oxford and Cambridge* (SCM, London, 1964), p. 235.
74 *Hansard Parliamentary Debates*, House of Commons (26 March 1834), vol. 22, col. 701.

contrary we affirm, that, if any person come to the service of the Church with a truly spiritual mind, he will find in our Liturgy what is calculated to call forth the devoutest exercises of his mind far more than in any of the extemporaneous prayers which he would hear in other places.

We forbear to enter into a fuller elucidation of this point at present, because we should detain you too long, and we shall have a better opportunity of doing it in our next Discourse. But we would here intreat you all so far to bear this objection in your minds, as to cut off all occasion for it as much as possible, and, by the devout manner of your attendance on the services of the Church, to shew, that though you worship God with a form, you also worship him in spirit and in truth. Dissenters themselves know that the repetition of favourite hymns does not generate formality; and they may from thence learn that the repetition of our excellent Liturgy is not really open to that objection. But they will judge from what they see amongst us: If they see that the prayers are read amongst us without any devotion, and that those who hear them, are inattentive and irreverent during the service, they will not impute these evils to the true and proper cause, but to the Liturgy itself: and it is a fact, that they do from this very circumstance derive great advantage for the weakening of men's attachment to the Established Church, and for the augmenting of their own societies. Surely then it becomes us who are annually sending forth so many ministers into every quarter of the land, to pay particular attention to this point. I am well aware that where such multitudes of young men are, it is not possible so to control the inconsiderateness of youth, as to suppress all levity, or to maintain that complete order that might be wished; but I know also that the ingenuousness of youth is open to conviction upon a subject like this, and that even the strictest discipline upon a point so interwoven with the honour of the Establishment and the eternal interests of their own souls, would, in a little time, meet with a more cordial concurrence than is generally imagined: it would commend itself to their consciences, and call forth, not only their present approbation, but their lasting gratitude: and if those who are in authority amongst us would lay this matter to heart, and devise means for the carrying it into full effect, more would be done for the upholding of the Establishment, than by ten thousand discourses in vindication of it: and verily, if but the smallest progress should be made in it, I should think that I had 'not laboured in vain, or run in vain'.

But let us not so think of the Establishment as to forget our own souls: for, after all, the great question for the consideration of us all is, Whether we ourselves are accepted in the use of these prayers? And here, it is not outward reverence and decorum that will suffice; the heart must be engaged, as well as the lips. It will be to little purpose that God say respecting us, 'They have well said all that they have spoken', unless he see his own wish also accomplished, 'O that there were in them such an heart!' Indeed our prayers will be no more than a solemn mockery, if there be not a correspondence between the words of our lips and the feeling of our own souls: and his answer to us will be, like that to the Jews of old, 'Ye hypocrites, in vain do ye worship me.' Let all of us then bring our devotions to this test, and look well to it, that, with 'the form, we have also the power of godliness.' We are too apt to rush into the Divine presence without any consciousness of the importance of the work in which we are going to be engaged, or any fear of his Majesty, whom we are going to address. If we would prevent formality in the house of God, we should endeavour to carry thither a devout spirit along with us, and guard against the very first incursion of vain thoughts and foolish imaginations. Let us then labour to attain such a sense of our own necessities and of God's unbounded goodness as shall produce a fixedness of mind, whenever we draw nigh to God in prayer; and for this end, let us ask of God the gift of his Holy Spirit to help our infirmities: and let us never think that we have used the Liturgy to any good purpose, unless it bring into our bosoms an inward witness of its utility, and a reasonable evidence of our acceptance with God in the use of it.[75]

---

75 Simeon, *The Excellency of the Liturgy* (1812), pp. 52–6.

Sermon III

Simeon's third sermon in the series turned positively to an exposition of the 'excellencies' of the Church of England's liturgy, and is reproduced here in full (apart from his discursus on the Athanasian Creed):[76]

In our preceding Discourses on this text, we first entered distinctly and fully into its true import, and then applied it, in an accommodated sense, to the Liturgy of our Established Church. The utility of a Liturgy being doubted by many, we endeavoured to vindicate the use of it, as lawful in itself, expedient for us, and acceptable to God. But it is not a mere vindication only which such a composition merits at our hands: the labour bestowed upon it has been exceeding great: Our first Reformers omitted nothing that could conduce to the improvement of it: they consulted the most pious and learned of foreign Divines, and submitted it to them for their correction: and, since their time, there have been frequent revisions of it, in order that every expression which could be made a subject of cavil, might be amended: by which means it has been brought to such a state of perfection, as no human composition of equal size and variety can pretend to.

To display its excellence is the task, which agreeably to the plan before proposed, is now assigned us; and we enter upon it with pleasure; in the hope, that those who have never yet studied the Liturgy, will learn to appreciate its value, and that all of us may be led to a more thankful and profitable use of it in future.

To judge of the Liturgy aright, we should contemplate *Its spirituality and purity – Its fulness and suitableness – Its moderation and candour.*

1st, Its spirituality and purity.

It is well known that the services of the Church of Rome, from whose communion we separated, were full of superstition and error: they taught the people to rest in carnal ordinances, without either stimulating them to real piety, or establishing them on the foundation which God has laid. They contained, it is true, much that was good;

---

76 *Ibid.,* pp. 57–82.

but they were at the same time so filled with ceremonies of man's invention, and with doctrines repugnant to the Gospel, that they tended only to deceive and ruin all who adhered to them. In direct opposition to those services, we affirm, that the whole scope and tendency of our Liturgy is to raise our minds to a holy and heavenly state, and to build us up upon the Lord Jesus Christ as the only foundation of a sinner's hope.

Let us look at the *stated* services of our Church; let us call to mind all that we have heard or uttered, from the introductory sentences which were to prepare our minds, to the Dismission Prayer which closes the whole; there is nothing for shew, but all for edification and spiritual improvement. Is humility the foundation of true piety? What deep humiliation is expressed in the General Confession, and throughout the Litany, as also in supplicating forgiveness after every one of the Commandments for our innumerable violations of them all! Is faith in the Lord Jesus Christ the way appointed for our reconciliation with God? We ask for every blessing solely in his Name and for his sake; and with the holy vehemence of importunity we urge with him the consideration of all that he has done and suffered for us, as our plea for mercy; and, at the Lord's Supper, we mark so fully our affiance in his atoning blood, that it is impossible for any one to use those prayers aright, without seeing and feeling that 'there is no other name under heaven but his, whereby we can be saved'.

The same we may observe respecting the *occasional* service of our Church. From our very birth even to the grave, our Church omits nothing that can tend to the edification of its members. At our first introduction into the Church, with what solemnity are we dedicated to God in our Baptismal Service! What pledges does our Church require of our Sponsors that we shall be brought up in the true faith and fear of God; and how earnestly does she lead us to pray for a progressive, total, and permanent renovation of our souls! No sooner are we capable of receiving instruction than she provides for us, and expressly requires that we be well instructed in, a Catechism, so short that it burthens the memory of none, and so comprehensive that it contains all that is necessary for our information at that early period of our life. When once we are taught by that to know the nature and extent of our baptismal vows, the Church calls upon us to renew in our own person the vows that were formerly made for us in our name; and, in a service specially prepared for that purpose, leads us to consecrate ourselves to God; thus endeavouring to *confirm* us in our holy resolutions, and to establish us in the faith of Christ. Not content with having thus initiated, instructed, and confirmed her members in the religion of Christ, the Church embraces every occasion of instilling into our minds the knowledge and love of his ways. If we change our condition in life, we are required to come to the altar of our God, and there devote ourselves afresh to him, and implore his blessing, from which alone all true happiness proceeds. Are mercies and deliverances vouchsafed to any, especially that great mercy of preservation from the pangs and perils of child-birth? the Church appoints a public acknowledgement to be made to Almighty God in the presence of the whole congregation, and provides a suitable service for that end. In like manner, for every public mercy, or in time of any public calamity, particular prayers and thanksgivings are provided for our use. In a time of sickness there is also very particular provision made for our instruction and consolation: and even after death, when she can no more benefit the deceased, the Church labours to promote the benefit of her surviving members, by a service the most solemn and impressive that ever was formed. Thus attentive is she to supply in every thing, as far as human endeavours can avail, our spiritual wants; being decent in her forms, but not superstitious; and strong in her expressions, but not erroneous. In short, it is not possible to read the Liturgy with candour, and not to see that the welfare of our souls is the one object of the whole; and that the compilers of it had nothing in view, but that in all our works begun, continued, and ended in God, we should glorify his holy Name.

The excellencies of our Liturgy will yet further appear while we notice, next, its *fulness and suitableness*.

Astonishing is the wisdom with which the Liturgy is adapted to the edification of every member of the Church. There is no case that is overlooked, no sin that is not deplored, no want that is not specified, no blessing that is not asked: yet, whilst every particular is entered into so far that every individual person may find his own case adverted to, and his own wishes expressed, the whole is so carefully worded, that no person is led to express more than he ought to feel, or to deliver sentiments, in which he may not join with his whole heart. Indeed there is a minuteness in the petitions that is rarely found even in men's private devotions; and those very particularities are founded in the deepest knowledge of the human heart, and the completest view of men's spiritual necessities: for instance, We pray to God to deliver us, not only in all time of our tribulation, but *in all time of our wealth also*; because we are quite as much in danger of being drawn from God by prosperity, as by adversity; and need his aid as much in the one as in the other.

In the intercessory part of our devotions also, our sympathy is called forth in behalf of all orders and degrees of men, under every name, and every character that can be conceived. We pray to him to strengthen *such as do stand*, to comfort and help *the weak-hearted*, and to raise up *them that fall*, and finally, to beat down Satan under our feet. We intreat him also to succour, help, and comfort *all that are in danger, necessity, and tribulation*. We further supplicate him in behalf of *all that travel*, whether *by land or water*, all *women labouring of child*, all *sick persons*, and *young children*, and particularly intreat him to have pity upon all *prisoners* and *captives*. Still further, we plead with him to defend and provide for the *fatherless children*, and *widows*, and *all that are desolate and oppressed*: and, lest any should have been omitted, we beg him 'to have mercy upon *all men*', generally, and more particularly 'to forgive our *enemies, persecutors*, and *slanderers*, and to turn their hearts'. In what other prayers, whether extemporaneous or written, shall we ever find such diffusive benevolence as this?

In a word, there is no possible situation in which we can be placed, but the prayers are precisely suited to us; nor can we be in any frame of mind wherein they will not express our feelings as strongly and forcibly, as any person could express them even in his secret chamber. Take a broken-hearted penitent; where can he ever find words, wherein to supplicate the mercy of his God, more congenial with his feelings than in the Litany, where he renews his application to each person of the Sacred Trinity for mercy, under the character of a miserable sinner? Hear him when kneeling before the altar of his God: 'Almighty God, Father of our Lord Jesus Christ, Maker of all things, Judge of all men, we acknowledge and bewail our manifold sins and wickedness which we from time to time most grievously have committed, by thought, word, and deed, against thy Divine Majesty, provoking most justly thy wrath and indignation against us. We do earnestly repent, and are heartily sorry for these our misdoings: the remembrance of them is grievous unto us; the burthen of them is intolerable. Have mercy upon us; have mercy upon us, most merciful Father: for thy Son our Lord Jesus Christ's sake, forgive us all that is past; and grant that we may ever hereafter serve and please thee in newness of life, to the honour and glory of thy Name, through Jesus Christ our Lord.' I may venture to say that no finite wisdom could suggest words more suited to the feelings or necessities of a penitent, than these.

Take, next, a person full of faith and of the Holy Ghost, and if he were the devoutest of all the human race, he could never find words wherein to give scope to all the exercises of his mind more suitable than in the *Te Deum*: 'We praise thee, O God, we acknowledge thee to be the Lord. All the earth doth worship thee, the Father everlasting. To thee all angels cry aloud, the heavens, and all the powers therein: To thee Cherubin and Seraphin continually do cry, Holy, Holy, Holy, Lord God of Sabaoth; Heaven and earth are full of the Majesty of thy glory.' Hear him also at the table of the Lord: 'It is very meet, right, and our bounden duty, that we should at all times and in all places give thanks unto thee, O Lord, holy Father, almighty, everlasting God: Therefore with angels and archangels, and with all the company of heaven, we laud and magnify thy glorious Name, evermore praising thee, and saying, Holy, Holy, Holy, Lord God of hosts, heaven and earth are full of thy glory; glory be to thee, O Lord most High.'

Even where there are no particular exercises of the mind, the Liturgy is calculated to produce the greatest possible good: for the gravity and sobriety of the whole service are fitted to impress the most careless sinner; whilst the various portions of Scripture that are read out of the Old and New Testament, not only for the Lessons of the day, but from the Psalms also, and from the Epistles and Gospels, are well adapted to arrest the attention of the thoughtless, and to convey instruction to the most ignorant. Indeed I consider it as one of the highest excellencies of our Liturgy, that it is calculated to make us wise, intelligent, and sober Christians: it marks a golden mean; it affects and inspires a meek, humble, modest, sober piety, equally remote from the coldness of a formalist, the self-importance of a systematic dogmatist, and the unhallowed fervour of a wild enthusiast. A *tender seriousness*, a *meek devotion*, and a *humble joy* are the qualities which it was intended, and is calculated, to produce in all her members.

It remains that we yet further trace the excellence of our Liturgy in its *Moderation and Candour*.

The whole Christian world has from time to time been agitated with controversies of different kinds; and human passions have grievously debased the characters and actions even of good men in every age. But it should seem that the compilers of our Liturgy were inspired with a wisdom and moderation peculiar to themselves. They kept back no truth whatever through fear of giving offence; yet were careful so to state every truth, as to leave those inexcusable who should recede from the Church on account of any sentiments which she maintained. In this they imitated the inspired penmen; who do not dwell on doctrines after the manner of human systems, but introduce them incidentally, as it were, as occasion suggests, and bring them forward always in connexion with practical duties. The various perfections of God are all stated in different parts; but all in such a way as, without affording any occasion for dispute, tends effectually to encourage us in our addresses to him. The Godhead of Christ is constantly asserted, and different prayers are expressly addressed to him; but nothing is said in a way of contentious disputation. The influences of the Holy Spirit, from whom all holy desires, all good counsels, and all just works do proceed, are stated; and 'the inspiration of the Holy Spirit is sought, in order that we may perfectly love God, and worthily magnify his holy Name': but all is conveyed in a way of humble devotion, without reflections upon others, or even a word that can lead the thoughts to controversy of any kind. Even the deepest doctrines of our holy religion are occasionally brought forth in a practical view (in which view alone they ought to be regarded); that, whilst we contemplate them as truths, we may experience their sanctifying efficacy on our hearts. The truth, the whole truth, is brought forward, without fear; but it is brought forward also without offence: all is temperate; all is candid; all is practical; all is peaceful; and every word is spoken in love. This is an excellency that deserves particular notice, because it is so contrary to what is found in the worship of those, whose addresses to the Most High God depend on the immediate views and feelings of an individual person, which may be, and not unfrequently are, tinctured in a lamentable degree by party-views, and unhallowed passions. And we shall do well to bear in mind this excellency, in order that we may imitate it; and that we may shew to all, that the moderation which so eminently characterizes the Offices of our Church, is no less visible in all her members.

Sorry should I be when speaking on this amiable virtue, to transgress it even in the smallest degree: but I appeal to all who hear me, whether there be not a want of this virtue in the temper of the present times; and whether, if our Reformers themselves were to rise again and live amongst us, their pious sentiments and holy lives would not be with many an occasion of offence? I need not repeat the terms which are used to stigmatize those who labour to walk in their paths; nor will I speak of the jealousies which are entertained against those, who live only to inculcate what our Reformers taught. You need not be told that even the moderate sentiments of our Reformers are at this day condemned by many as dangerous errors; and the very exertions, whereby alone the knowledge of them can be communicated unto men, are imputed to vanity and loaded with blame. But, though I thus speak, I must acknowledge to the glory of God, that in no place have moderation and candour shone more conspicuous, than in this distinguished seat of literature and science: and I pray God, that the exercise of these virtues may be richly recompensed from the Lord into every bosom, and be followed with all the other graces that accompany salvation.

From this view of our subject it will be naturally asked, Do I then consider the Liturgy as altogether perfect? I answer, No: it is a human composition; and there is nothing human than can claim so high a title as that of absolute perfection. There are certainly some few expressions which might be altered for the better, and which in all probability would have been altered at the Conference which was appointed for the last revision of it, if the unreasonable scrupulosity of some, and the unbending pertinacity of others, had not defeated the object of that assembly.[77] I have before mentioned two, which, though capable of being vindicated, might admit of some improvement. And, as I have been speaking strongly of the moderation and candour of the Liturgy, I will here bring forward the only exception to it that I am aware of; and that is found in the Athanasian Creed. The damnatory clauses contained in that Creed, do certainly breathe a very different spirit from that which pervades every other part of our Liturgy. As to the doctrine of the Creed, it is perfectly sound, and such as ought to be universally received. But it is a matter of regret that any should be led to pronounce a sentence of damnation against their fellow-creatures, in any case where God himself has not clearly and certainly pronounced it. Yet whilst I say this, permit me to add, that I think this Creed does not express, nor ever was intended to express, so much as is generally supposed. ...[78] Still, after all, I confess, that if the same candour and moderation that are observable in all other parts of the Liturgy, had been preserved here, it would have been better. For though I do verily believe, that those who deny the doctrine

---

77 That is, the Savoy Conference of 1661.

78 Here Simeon went on to discuss the damnatory clauses of the Athanasian Creed, the sole part of the Sermon omitted here; *ibid.*, pp. 72–6.

of the Trinity, are in a fatal error, and will find themselves so at the day of judgment, I would rather deplore the curse that awaits then, than denounce it; and rather weep over them in my secret chamber, than utter anathemas against them in the house of God.

I hope I have now met the question of our Liturgy fairly. I have not confined myself to general assertions, but have set forth the difficulties which are supposed to exist against it, and have given such a solution of them, as I think is sufficient to satisfy any conscientious mind: though it is still matter of regret that any laboured explanation of them should be necessary.

Now then, acknowledging that our Liturgy is not absolutely perfect, and that those who most admire it would be glad if these few blemishes were removed; have we not still abundant reason to be thankful for it? Let its excellencies be fairly weighed; and its blemishes will sink into nothing: let its excellencies be duly appreciated, and every person in the kingdom will acknowledge himself deeply indebted to those, who with so much care and piety compiled it.

But these blemishes *alone* are seen by multitudes; and its excellencies are altogether forgotten: yea, moreover, frequent occasion is taken from these blemishes to persuade men to renounce their communion with the Established Church, in the hopes of finding a purer worship elsewhere. With what justice such arguments are urged, will best appear by a comparison between the prayers that are offered elsewhere, and those that are offered in the Established Church. There are about 11,000 places of worship in the Established Church, and about as many out of it. Now take the prayers that are offered on any sabbath in all places out of the Establishment; have them all written down, and every expression sifted and scrutinized as our Liturgy has been: then compare them with the prayers that have been offered in all the Churches of the kingdom; and see what comparison the extemporaneous effusions will bear with our pre-composed forms. Having done this for *one sabbath*, proceed to do it for *a year*; and then, after a similar examination, compare them again: were this done, (and done it ought to be in order to form a correct judgment on the case), methinks there is scarcely a man in the kingdom that would not fall down on his knees and bless God for the Liturgy of the Established Church.

All that is wanting is, *an heart suited to the Liturgy*, and cast as it were into that mould. It may with truth be said of us, 'They have well said all that they have spoken: O that there were in them such an heart!' Let us only suppose that on any particular occasion there were in all of us such a state of mind as the Liturgy is suited to express; what glorious worship would ours be! and how certainly would God delight to hear and bless us! We will not say that he would come down and fill the house with his visible glory, as he did in the days of Moses and of Solomon; but we will say, that he would come down and fill our souls with such a sense of his presence and love, as would transform us into his blessed image, and constitute a very heaven upon earth. Let each of us then adopt the wish in our text, and say, 'O that there *may be* in *me* such an heart!' Let us cultivate the *moderation and candour* which are there exhibited; divesting ourselves of all prejudice against religion, and receiving with impartial readiness the whole counsel of our God. More particularly, whenever we come up to the house of God, let us seek those very dispositions in the use of the Liturgy, which our Reformers exercised in the framing of it. Let us bring with us into the presence of our God that *spirituality of mind* that shall fit us for communion with him, and that *purity of heart* which is the commencement of the Divine image on the soul. Let us study, whenever we join in the different parts of this Liturgy, to get our heart *suitably impressed* with the work in which we are engaged; that our confessions may be humble, our petitions fervent, our thanksgivings devout, and our whole souls obedient to the word we hear. In a word, let us not be satisfied with any attainments, but labour to be holy as God himself is holy, and perfect even as our Father which is in heaven is perfect. If now a doubt remain on the mind of any individual respecting the transcendent excellence of the Liturgy, let him only take the Litany, and go through every petition of it attentively, and at the close of every petition ask himself, What sort of a person should I be, if this petition were so answered to me, that I lived henceforth according to it? and what kind of a world would this be, if all the people that were in it experienced the same answer, and walked according to the same model? If, for instance, we were all from this hour delivered 'from all blindness of heart; from pride, vain-glory, and hypocrisy; from envy, hatred, and malice, and all uncharitableness'; if we were delivered also 'from all other deadly sin, and from all the deceits of the world, the flesh, and the devil'; what happiness should we not possess? How happy would *the Church* be, if it should 'please God to illuminate all bishops, priests, and deacons with true knowledge and understanding of his word, so that both by their preaching and living they did set it forth and shew it accordingly!' How blessed also would *the whole nation* be, if it pleased God to 'endue the Lords of the Council, and all the nobility, with grace, wisdom, and understanding: and to bless and keep the magistrates, giving them grace to execute justice and to maintain truth; and further to bless all his people throughout the land!' Yea, what *a world* would this be, if from this moment God should 'give to all nations unity, peace, and concord!' Were these prayers once answered, we should hear no more complaints of our Liturgy, nor ever wish for any thing *in public*, better than that which is provided for us. May God hasten forward that happy day, when all the assemblies of his people throughout the land shall enter full into the spirit of these prayers, and be answered in the desire of their hearts; receiving from him an 'increase of grace, to hear meekly his word, to receive it with pure affection, and to bring forth the fruits of the Spirit!' And to us in particular may he give, even to every individual amongst us, 'true repentance; and forgive us all our sins, negligences, and ignorances; and endue us with the grace of his Holy Spirit, that we may amend our lives according to his holy word.' Amen and Amen.

Sermon IV

Simeon's congregation at the University Church in Cambridge was dominated by clergymen and (amongst the undergraduates) future clergymen. Therefore in his fourth and final sermon on the Liturgy he chose to focus upon the excellencies of the Ordination Service. He began:

> The further we proceed in the investigation of our Liturgy, the more we feel the difficulty of doing justice to it. Such is the spirit which it breathes throughout, that if only a small measure of its piety existed in all the different congregations in which it is used, we should be as holy and as happy a people, as ever the Jews were in the most distinguished periods of their history. If this object has not been yet attained, it is not the fault of our Reformers: they have done all that men could do, to transmit to the latest posterity the blessings which they themselves received: and there is not a member of our Church, who has not reason to bless God every day of his life for their labours. But they knew that it would be to little purpose to provide suitable form of prayer for every different occasion, if they did not also secure, as far as human wisdom could secure, a succession of men, who, actuated by the same ardent piety as themselves, should perform the different offices to the greatest advantage, and carry on by their personal ministrations the blessed work which *they* had begun. Here therefore they bestowed the utmost care; marking with precision what were the qualifications requisite for the ministerial office, and binding in the most solemn manner all who should be consecrated to it, to a diligent and faithful discharge of their respective duties.[79]

Simeon then proceeded to expound the Ordination Service in detail, observing that any discussion of the merits of the Liturgy would be incomplete if he omitted that part 'which so pre-eminently displays its highest excellencies, and is peculiarly appropriate to the audience which I have the honour to address'.[80] He focussed upon the bishop's exhortation to ordination candidates, recommending that every minister read it at least once every year. From this portion of the Liturgy, Simeon

---

79 *Ibid.*, pp. 83–4.
80 *Ibid.*, p. 85.

drew out three major themes – the privilege of Christian ministry, its vital importance, and the strenuous effort needed to fulfil the charge. These he enthusiastically hammered home to the congregation, declaring:

> Now, if we occupied such an office in the house of an earthly monarch only, our dignity were great; but to be thus engaged in the service of the Kings of kings, is an honour far greater than the temporal government of the whole universe.[81]

> What bounds would there be to our exertions, if we considered as we ought, that we are engaged in that very work, for which our Lord Jesus Christ came down from the bosom of his Father, and shed his blood upon the cross; and that to us he looks for the completion of his efforts in the salvation of a ruined world?[82]

> The careless minister may spend many years in a populous parish, and yet never see one sinner converted from the error of his ways, or turned unto God in newness of life. But the faithful servant of Jehovah will have some fruit of his ministry. ... What if all *prayed* the prayers instead of reading them; and laboured *out of the pulpit* as well as in it ... Only let us be faithful to our engagements, and our Churches will be crowded, our Sacraments thronged, our hearers edified: good institutions will be set on foot; liberality will be exercised, the poor benefited, the ignorant enlightened, the distressed comforted; yea, our 'wilderness world will rejoice and blossom as the rose'. O that we might see this happy day; which, I would fondly hope, has begun to dawn![83]

Simeon concluded his sermon, and his series, with the bold statement

---

81 *Ibid.*, pp. 91–2.
82 *Ibid.*, p. 92.
83 *Ibid.*, pp. 107–10.

that the Liturgy itself would 'appear against us in judgment, if we labour not to the utmost of our power to fulfil the engagements which we have voluntarily entered into: Yea, God himself will say to us, "Out of thine own mouth will I judge thee, thou wicked servant." May God enable us all to lay these things to heart …'[84]

---

84 *Ibid.*, p. 111.

3

Engulfed in Controversy

Simeon had no intention of publishing his sermons on *The Excellency of the Liturgy* for a few years at least, until his *Horae Homileticae* was ready for the press. They were meant to stand at the head of this *magnum opus*. However, in the midst of fresh controversy in Cambridge, he was forced to change his mind and quickly issued them for wide circulation. Before his fourth and final sermon had been delivered, agitation was already beginning to boil over concerning the role of the British and Foreign Bible Society. For several months the University was embroiled in heated debate, much of which centred upon the relationship between the Bible and the *Book of Common Prayer*. In this new context, Simeon's sermons took on an extra significance.

In 1804 evangelicals within the Church of England had joined forces with their Nonconformist friends to establish the British and Foreign Bible Society, a pan-evangelical organization whose single purpose was to distribute Bibles worldwide. Unlike the long-established Anglican organization, the Society for Promoting Christian Knowledge (founded in 1698), which distributed a wide variety of literature including Bibles and Prayer Books, the Bible Society deliberately limited its mission to Bibles without any additional commentary.[85] The new group was

---

85 On this background, see Roger H. Martin, *Evangelicals United: Ecumenical Stirrings in Pre-Victorian Britain, 1795–1830* (Scarecrow Press, Metuchen, NJ, 1983), chs 5–7; Leslie Howsam, *Cheap Bibles: Nineteenth-Century Publishing and the British and Foreign Bible Society* (Cambridge University Press, Cambridge, 1991), chs 1–2; W. K. Lowther Clarke, *A History of the S.P.C.K.* (SPCK, London, 1959).

dominated by Anglicans, and enjoyed wide episcopal patronage, but was open to all. It experienced phenomenal growth, with local auxiliaries soon set up in towns and cities across Britain from 1809, and Simeon was a driving force behind the launch of a Cambridge auxiliary in 1811. In the middle of his final sermon on *The Excellency of the Liturgy*, while expounding the Ordination Service, Simeon interjected:

Here let us pause a moment, to reflect, what stress our Reformers laid on the Holy Scriptures, as the only sure directory for our faith and practice, and the only certain rule of all our ministrations. They have clearly given it as their sentiment, that to study the word of God ourselves, and to open it to others, is the proper labour of a minister; a labour, that calls for all his time, and all his attention: and, by this zeal of theirs in behalf of the Inspired Volume, they were happily successful in bringing it into general use. But, if they could look down upon us at this time, and see what an unprecedented zeal has pervaded all ranks and orders of men amongst us for the dissemination of that truth, which they, at the expence of their own lives, transmitted to us; how would they rejoice and leap for joy! Yet, methinks, if they cast an eye upon this favoured spot,[86] and saw, that, whilst the Lord Jesus Christ is thus exalted in almost every other place, we are lukewarm in his cause; and whilst thousands all around us are emulating each other in exertions to extend his kingdom through the world, we, who are so liberal on other occasions, have not yet appeared in his favour; they would be ready to rebuke our tardiness, as David did the indifference of Judah, from whom he had reason to expect the most active support; 'Why are ye the last to bring the king back to his house, seeing the speech of all Israel is come to the king, even to his house?' But I am persuaded, that there is nothing wanting but that a suitable proposal be made by some person of influence amongst us; and we shall soon approve ourselves worthy sons of those pious ancestors: I would hope there is not an individual amongst us, who would not gladly lend his

---

86 That is, Cambridge University.

aid, that 'the word of the Lord may run and be glorified', not in this kingdom only, but, if possible, throughout all the earth.[87]

Here was a clear exhortation, from Cambridge's most significant pulpit, for the University to throw its weight behind Bible distribution. Yet the Bible Society was strongly opposed by a powerful lobby within the University.[88] Their spokesman was Simeon's old antagonist, Professor Herbert Marsh, who issued an address to the University's Senate proclaiming that to support the SPCK ('the *ancient* Bible Society') was to uphold the Church of England, but to support the Bible Society was to undermine the Church of England.[89] It was the 'indispensable duty' of Churchmen to follow the SPCK's lead and distribute the Bible and the Prayer Book together, so that recipients would know how to interpret the Scriptures correctly:

> though in the spirit of true Protestantism it acknowledges the Bible as the only *fountain* of religious truth, yet, it knows from the experience of all ages, that the waters of that fountain will be clear or turbid, according to the channel into which they are drawn.

In contrast, Marsh observed, the Bible Society left Bible readers to come to their own doctrinal conclusions and ignored denominational distinctives. This policy would lead to the 'evident danger, that the pre-eminence of the *established religion* should be gradually forgotten, and finally lost'. It might even result in the 'dissolution' of the Church of England:

> Now if we injure, or even neglect to support *our own* Church, we shall hardly make compensation by our distribution of Bibles in *foreign*

---

87 Simeon, *The Excellency of the Liturgy* (1812), pp. 96–7.

88 On the Cambridge controversy, see especially Ford K. Brown, *Fathers of the Victorians: The Age of Wilberforce* (Cambridge University Press, Cambridge, 1961), ch. 8.

89 Herbert Marsh, *An Address to the Members of the Senate of the University of Cambridge; Occasioned by the Proposal to Introduce in this Place an Auxiliary Bible Society* (Cambridge, 1811).

parts. If *our own* Church, as we have reason to believe, professes Christianity in its *purest* form, the downfall of *such* a Church would be an irreparable loss, not to *this* nation only, but to the *whole world*.

One bemused correspondent replied to Marsh's protests: 'I am wholly unable to see how the extensive circulation of the Bible can possibly injure the Church of England.'[90] Likewise Nicholas Vansittart (a vice-president of the Bible Society, and Chancellor of the Exchequer from 1812) tried to deflect the criticism: 'I should, as a member of the Church, be very sorry to think that the devout study of the Scriptures could lead to the disregard of our Liturgy; on the contrary, I should hope that it would produce a more general acknowledgement of its excellence.'[91] At the launch event of the Cambridge auxiliary in the Town Hall on 12 December, Marsh's position was derided. For example, his fellow professor, Edward Clarke (Professor of Mineralogy) asked:

> Is the distribution of the Bible *alone* detrimental to the interests of the establishment? Have we forgot that we are Englishmen? Have we forgot that we are PROTESTANTS? What would Latimer, and Ridley, and Chillingworth have thought, or said, had they lived unto this day to bear testimony to such a declaration?[92]

Professor Marsh returned to the assault the following month with his treatise, *An Inquiry into the Consequences of Neglecting to Give the Prayer Book with the Bible*. Again he reiterated that to distribute the Bible alone was 'a dereliction of our duty as Churchmen',[93] because the *Book of Common Prayer* was needed to provide a doctrinal framework for the Bible's interpretation:

---

90 *Christian Observer* vol. 10 (December 1811), p. 797.

91 Nicholas Vansittart, *Letter to the Rev Dr Marsh* (Gosnell, London, 1811), p. 4.

92 William Farish (ed.), *A Report on the Formation of the Cambridge Auxiliary Bible Society* (Hodson, Cambridge, 1812), p. 19.

93 Herbert Marsh, *An Inquiry into the Consequences of Neglecting to Give the Prayer Book with the Bible, Interspersed with Remarks on Some Late Speeches at Cambridge, and Other Important Matter Relative to the British and Foreign Bible Society* (Deighton, Cambridge, 1812), p. 6.

When we further consider, that there is at present hardly a town, or even a village, which is not visited by illiterate teachers, who expound the Bible with more confidence than the most profound theologian, it becomes *doubly* necessary, if we would preserve the poor of the establishment in the religion of their fathers, to provide them with a safeguard against the delusions of *false interpretation*. And what better safeguard *can* we offer than the Book of Common Prayer, which contains the doctrines of the Bible, according to its *true* exposition ...[94]

Many were quoting William Chillingworth's famous motto that 'The Bible alone is the religion of Protestants', yet Marsh observed that Chillingworth was merely a proponent of '*generalized* Protestantism' devoid of a particular creed. The Bible might make people Protestants, but by itself it could not make them into the right sort of Protestants:

the *Bible only* is the religion of the *Protestant*. But are all Protestants *alike* in their religion? Have we not Protestants of the Church of England, Protestants of the Church of Scotland, Protestants who hold the confession of Augsburg? Have we not both Arminian and Calvinistic Protestants? Are not the Moravians, the Methodists, the Baptists, the Quakers, and even the Jumpers, the Dunkers, and Swedenborgians all *Protestants*?[95]

The professor went further and drew parallels between the Puritans of the Westminster Assembly in the 1640s who had abolished the *Book of Common Prayer*, and the 'Calvinistic' (for which read 'evangelical') clergy of the 1810s who were campaigning on behalf of the Bible Society. He warned:

Now a man, who adopts the doctrines of Calvin, cannot be *zealously* attached to our English Liturgy. A Calvinist may in *many respects* have

---

94 *Ibid.*, p. 5.
95 *Ibid.*, p. 14.

a great regard for it: but he cannot have *much pain* in parting with it, as it abounds with passages so decisive of *conditional* salvation, that no ingenuity can torture them into the language of *absolute* decrees.[96]

He claimed that the Bible Society bred 'an indifference to the *Liturgy*' amongst Anglicans, which would lead to 'the ruin' of the Church of England, so they should transfer their allegiance to the SPCK, 'that true *Church of England* Society'.[97]

Marsh's polemic brought a heap of controversy upon his head. One of the first out of the blocks in reply was Charles Simeon, stung into action by the insinuation that Anglican evangelicals were disloyal to the Prayer Book. He quickly published his own sermons on *The Excellency of the Liturgy*, with *An Answer to Dr Marsh's Inquiry* as an extended preface, asserting: 'I contend for the *Liturgy*, as much as any man; but I object to the being represented as an enemy to it, because I do my utmost to promote, at home as well as abroad, the distribution of the *Bible*.'[98] It was simply false, Simeon insisted, to claim that the evangelical clergy neglected the Prayer Book: 'your whole argument from beginning to end is founded on a FACT, *not proved, not supported, not defensible, not true*.'[99] He protested at length that evangelicals *en masse* were being misrepresented and stigmatized as 'Calvinistic', an 'injurious and obnoxious' title, and maintained that they preached only what is 'perfectly in harmony with the Articles, the Homilies, and the Liturgy of the Church of England',[100] defying the whole world to contradict him.

As proof of Anglican evangelical zeal for the Prayer Book, Simeon pointed to his own sermons before the University – both *The Churchman's Confession* and his recent series on *The Excellency of the Liturgy*. With these in view he issued the stark challenge with which this

---

96 *Ibid.*, p. 48.

97 *Ibid.*, pp. 58, 62.

98 Charles Simeon, *The Excellency of the Liturgy in Four Discourses … to which is prefixed An Answer to Dr Marsh's Inquiry* (Smith, Cambridge, 1812), p. 4.

99 *Ibid.*, pp. 7–8.

100 *Ibid.*, pp. 12, 29–30.

booklet began: 'I desire every thing I ever have written, or ever shall write, to be brought to *that test*, THE LITURGY OF THE CHURCH OF ENGLAND; persuaded as I am of its perfect conformity to the Holy Scriptures.'[101] Warming to his theme, Simeon continued:

> But, Sir, I will not rest satisfied with assertions: I will bring you proofs. Inquire as extensively and minutely as you can, who among the Clergy are they that are continually *making their appeal to* the Articles, the Homilies, and the Liturgy of the Church of England? Who are they that *write and preach Expositions* of the Liturgy? Who are they that *read the Homilies* to their congregations? I will tell you, Sir, without fear of contradiction; they are the Clergy whom you *invidiously* call, 'The *Calvinistic* Clergy'.[102]

Simeon then proceeded to name Samuel Walker, Thomas Biddulph, Thomas Rogers and Basil Woodd as prominent examples of evangelical clergymen who had written in praise of the Prayer Book. Anglican members of the Bible Society were not only strongly attached to the Liturgy but in their zeal, he told Marsh, 'even outstripped those whom you suppose to have an exclusive claim to be called, The Friends of the Church.'[103]

The controversy flowed on for many months, with numerous replies and counter-replies pouring forth from various quarters, as theological combatants eagerly picked up their pens to defend or assail the Bible Society or Professor Marsh, and to wrangle over the relationship between the Bible and the *Book of Common Prayer*. Some were pungent pamphlets, others were verbose treatises like that by Simeon's friend, Isaac Milner (President of Queens' College, Cambridge and Dean of Carlisle), which ran to over four hundred pages.[104] In the midst of the

---

101 *Ibid.*, p. 34.
102 *Ibid.*, p. 36.
103 *Ibid.*, p. 56.
104 Isaac Milner, *Strictures on Some of the Publications of the Rev. Herbert Marsh, Intended as a Reply to his Objections Against the British and Foreign Bible Society* (Hatchard, London, 1813).

furore, Simeon and Marsh renewed their personal quarrel, clashing twice more in print.[105] The professor was soon worn down by the strength of the hostile reactions he had provoked, and concluded in some despair that resisting the Bible Society was 'like attempting to oppose a torrent of burning lava that issues from Etna or Vesuvius'.[106]

One of the most enduring and constructive results of the Cambridge controversy was the formation in May 1812 of the Prayer Book and Homily Society (PBHS), promoted by Anglican evangelical members of the British and Foreign Bible Society.[107] Its aim was worldwide distribution and translation of the *Book of Common Prayer* and the Anglican Homilies, partly in vindication of the Church of England's Reformation heritage, but also as a public demonstration of evangelical loyalty to the Liturgy since this had been thrown in doubt by Professor Marsh and others. From the platform of annual PBHS events, prominent Anglican evangelicals queued up to laud the Liturgy, and Simeon declared that this new society deserved 'the countenance and support of every pious man'.[108] On one such occasion, he spoke in fulsome praise of the Liturgy as a foretaste of heaven, when prayed in the right spirit by worshipping congregations. We will give Simeon the last word here, as an articulate summary of his position. Driving home the point already expounded at length in his sermons at Cambridge on *The Excellency of the Liturgy*, he proclaimed of the *Book of Common Prayer*:

> no commendation can be too great for it. Being of human composition, it must, of necessity, partake of human infirmity. But,

---

105 Charles Simeon, *Dr Marsh's Fact; or, A Congratulatory Address to the Church-Members of the British and Foreign Bible Society* (Hodson, Cambridge, 1813); Herbert Marsh, *A Letter to the Rev. Charles Simeon, in Answer to his Pretended Congratulatory Address* (Hodson, Cambridge, 1813); Charles Simeon, *Appendix to Dr Marsh's Fact* (Hodson, Cambridge, 1813); Herbert Marsh, *A Second Letter to the Rev. Charles Simeon, in Confutation of his Various Mis-Statements* (Hodson, Cambridge, 1813).

106 Herbert Marsh, *A Reply to the Strictures of the Rev. Isaac Milner* (Hodson, Cambridge, 1813), p. 141.

107 On the origins of the PBHS, see Gareth Atkins, 'Anglican Evangelicals and Reformation Literature, c.1770–1850' (unpublished paper).

108 'Forms of Prayer, Good', in Simeon, *Horae Homileticae*, vol. 12, p. 437.

taken all together, it comes nearer to inspiration than any book that ever was composed. Only let a person be humbled as a sinner before God, and he will not find in the whole universe any prayers so suited to his taste. They express exactly what a broken-hearted penitent before God would desire to express: yet is there in them nothing of extravagance or of cant: all is sober, chaste, judicious; so minute, as to comprehend every thing which the largest assembly of suppliants could wish to utter; and at the same time so general, as not to involve any one to a greater extent than his own experience sanctions and approves. Throughout the whole, the suppliant is made to stand on the only true foundation, and to urge every request in the name of the Lord Jesus Christ, his atoning Saviour, his all-prevailing Advocate. Throughout the whole, also, is the Holy Spirit's influence acknowledged as the only source of light and life, and implored as the gift of God to sinners for Christ's sake. In point of devotion, whether prayer or praise be offered, nothing can exceed the Liturgy, either in urgency of petition or in fervour of thanksgiving. In truth, if a whole assembly were addressing God in *the spirit of* the Liturgy, as well as in *the words*, there would be nothing to compare with such a spectacle upon the face of the earth: it would approximate more to heaven than any thing of the kind that was ever yet seen in this world.[109]

---

109 *Ibid.*, p. 437.

The Alcuin Club promotes the study of Christian Liturgy, especially the liturgy of the Anglican Communion. It has a long history of publishing an annual Collection, and has shared with GROW since 1987 in also publishing the Joint Liturgical Studies. Members receive all publications free. For details of membership contact: The Alcuin Club, St Anne's Vicarage, 182 St Ann's Hill, London SW18 2RS. Telephone: 0208 874 2809. E-mail: gordon.jeanes@stanneswandsworth.org.uk

The Group for Renewal of Worship (GROW) has for 40 years been a focus for forward-thinking, often adventurous, explorations in Anglican worship. It has produced (by its own members writing, or by its commissioning of others) over 200 titles in the Grove Worship Series, and until 1986 similarly produced Grove Liturgical Studies, many of which are still in print. Enquiries about GROW can sent to Grove Books Ltd, Ridley Hall Road, Cambridge CB3 9HU, or to members of the Group.

From 1987 to 2004, the Joint Editorial Board of the two sponsoring agencies commissioned numbers 1–58 of Joint Liturgical Studies, published by Grove Books Ltd (see the Grove Books website or end-pages of previous Joint Liturgical Studies). In 2005, SCM-Canterbury Press Ltd, now Hymns Ancient and Modern, became the publishers. Two titles (of 48–60 pages) are published each year. Copies are available at £6.95 from Hymns Ancient & Modern.

In 2012 no.73 will be *Ordo Romanus Primus: A Text for Students* translated and introduced by Alan Griffiths.

The current series of Joint Liturgical Studies is available through booksellers, on standing order either by joining the Alcuin Club (see above) or from Hymns Ancient and Modern, Subscription Office, 13a Hellesdon Park Road, Norwich, Norfolk NR6 5DR, UK, Telephone 01603 785910 or online at www.jointliturgicalstudies.co.uk.

HYMNS ANCIENT & MODERN
13a Hellesdon Park Road, Norwich, Norfolk NR6 5DR, UK
Telephone: 01603 785900 Fax: 01603 785915
e-mail: jls@hymnsam.co.uk

CPSIA information can be obtained
at www.ICGtesting.com
Printed in the USA
JSHW022052220222
23233JS00007B/121